The Great Railroad Race

Written by Bridie Dickson

Contents

Introduction

Once, the only way people could travel across the USA was by riding a horse or in a wagon pulled by horses.

People had to travel across deserts and over mountains. They could be attacked and killed by wild animals, and there were no towns to stop at and get food.

It was a long journey that took about six months and it was very unsafe.

Then, about 150 years ago, a railroad track was built across the USA.

Two teams worked on the railroad. One started on the west coast, and the other started in the east. The two teams raced each other to lay the most railroad track.

Building the railroad was hard work in dangerous conditions. It took over six years to build this railroad and hundreds of men died. It was built over snowy mountains and across hot, dry deserts. The men who built this railroad were brave and strong.

West
East
Sacramento
Omaha

Chapter 1

The railroad begins in the west

A team of workers started building the railroad on the west coast of the USA in 1863. They had to build the first section of the railroad across mountains.

The men had to work in freezing cold conditions. There were many blizzards and thick snow. Sometimes, huge amounts of snow, ice and rocks came tumbling down the mountain in an *avalanche*. Many men were injured.

It took two long years for the workers to build the first 40 miles of track. But they still had a long way to go.

The workers had to build tall, wooden bridges across wide, deep canyons. They had to blast through solid rock. Workers were lifted down the side of mountains in big baskets to plant explosives. They were pulled out quickly before the explosives went off. It was risky work.

EAST

After five years, the team from the west finally crossed the mountains. They had worked hard to build 50 bridges and 14 tunnels over a distance of 120 miles.

The worst was now behind them, and flat land lay ahead.

Chapter 2

The race is on from the east

Two years after the team from the west had started on the railroad, work began in the east of the USA.

In 1866, a team of railroad builders began laying track on flat land. They had a much easier start than the workers from the west. They built their first 40 miles of track in just one month.

After six months, the team from the east had built 250 miles of track. But then problems began for them, too.

The conditions in the camps where the workers lived were difficult. It was hard to get food and other supplies. Sometimes, the workers were hungry for days. Some workers gave up and left, but many stayed.

EAST

The railroad workers were also attacked by the Native Americans, who did not want the railroad built on their land.

Then it began to rain. It rained and rained, and there were floods. Miles of track were washed away, and even more workers left.

EAST

Chapter 3

Meeting in the middle

The two teams had many problems, but they worked long and hard to lay as much track as possible.

Soon, only 50 miles separated the two teams, and a finishing point was chosen. Both teams worked day and night to reach the finishing point.

On 30 April 1869, the team from the west reached the finishing point first! Two days later, the team from the east arrived.

Promontory Point in Utah was the finishing point where the two teams met.

EAST

On 10 May 1869, workers from both teams joined together to lay the last piece of track. The total length of the railroad was 1776 miles.

The trip across the USA now took seven days. The railroad made it possible to build towns and cities right across the country.

Many strong and brave people built this railroad, which remains one of America's most important achievements.

A note about measurements

This book uses the measurement of miles, not kilometres, to measure length. When the Union Pacific Railroad was built, miles were used to measure length. Today, miles are still used in the USA to measure length.

Here are the lengths in this story converted into kilometres.

Page number	Length in miles	Length in kilometres
10	40 miles	65 kilometres
12	120 miles	193 kilometres
14	40 miles	65 kilometres
16	250 miles	402 kilometres
22	1776 miles	2858 kilometres